Bias is All Around You:

A Handbook for Inspecting
Social Media & News Stories

BiasHandbook.com

HealthyMindExpress.org

ISBN: 978-1-7344744-1-1

Library of Congress Control Number: 2021940373

Written by Erik Bean, Ed.D.
Illustrations & Cover by Gail Gorske
Editor Sherry Wexler

Hardcover library acquisitions distributor Baker & Taylor
Call Healthy Mind Express 248-270-2974 for multiple book discounts.

Dedication

We dedicate this book to our forefathers who gave us the freedom of speech in the First Amendment of the United States Constitution. May this book lead everyone to partake in a more productive, civil discourse.

Table of Contents

Bias Is All Around You

FOREWORD Transparency has become an increasingly important social value in the 21st Century. Transparency is so welcome because it takes bias out of the shadows and into the full light of day. Transparency is fundamentally about openness. As a social value, it means that we should readily share information that is of public value and let people know how we arrived at our conclusions. It is important to be confident in our conclusions, and that we divulge what our own biases are. Then, others can make their own judgments about the matters that have been shared. Transparency is needed when bias is all around you. However, for at least a few reasons, transparency is not the solution to all of our problems.

First, the burden is now squarely on us as individuals to sift through information and take into consideration the who, how, and what went into the creation of that information before we arrive at our own conclusions. That's fine, but few of us are well prepared for the job. That's why this book is important. If transparency is going to be a helpful social value, all of us need to be much more attuned to the biases that are baked into the information we encounter nearly every moment of every day. We must be able to assess, for example, whether the process someone used to generate new information is truly valid and reliable.

Second, if the burden is on individuals, they will eventually run out of the capacity to investigate all the information that comes at them each day. If I want to know what important business was decided this week in the U.S. Senate and someone hands me thousands of pages of transcripts from the Congressional Record, that person has arguably been transparent. But that doesn't mean I have a clear and easy answer to my question. Of course, we used to rely on institutions, such as the news media, to help us with that job. But news media outlets often have their own biases. Many are even transparent about what those biases are. But, again, we must know how to assess those biases.

Third, if transparency is indeed a social value, pretty much everyone is going to claim they're being transparent. But that just means some will make the calculation that it is more to their advantage to feign transparency than to be transparent. People might say they have nothing to hide and still be hiding something. Again, that's why this book is important. We can't be tricked into thinking we're getting the whole picture just because someone seems willing to share information and answer questions.

Finally, it should be noted that not everyone is on board with transparency. For example, many of our online experiences are driven by what Silicon Valley algorithms calculate for us. These algorithms are almost never divulged to the public and calls for greater transparency go unheeded. Here it becomes important to know what we don't know.

All of this suggests we need to create mental habits to better filter and assess information. Twenty-First Century life, particularly in democratic societies, relies on everyone playing their part in the day-to-day assessment of information. It can be hard work. Especially at first. It's a lot like physical exercise – muscles that haven't had a regular workout hurt at first. But good mental health requires regular exercise. Our brains may hurt, but that can be a sign our mental abilities are getting stronger. This book will get you started on a healthy mental exercise routine to better assess information bias, strengthen your media literacy, and allow you to contribute to more meaningful civil discourse.

Cheers!

Tim Vos, Ph.D.
Director
School of Journalism
Michigan State University

INTRODUCTION "A life worth living is a life well led," as the famous saying goes. We need to take the lead in all aspects of our lives and that includes how we assess and interact with information. Inspecting information can improve your mental health. We are inundated with a barrage of seemingly unending and conflicting data. Information should be based on facts and designed to enrich our lives.

However, information can be misleading and contrived. The internet, television, radio, and social media networks provide us with minute-by-minute access to millions upon millions of bytes of data. And let's not forget to mention newspapers and magazines. We are also exposed to websites, blogs, podcasts, videos, and online libraries, and all of these avenues should increase our knowledge and provide us with a sense of direction. However, our comprehension of this information can be clumsy or simply inept.

If we do not properly inspect information, we can make hasty generalizations. We can then manipulate this material to our advantage without understanding the ramifications of sharing false narratives in the form of rumors and innuendo. Worse, we could possibly end up following a false cause because we were duped with misinformation. We are often unaware that much of the information we have access to is derived by social media manipulation and corporate digital algorithms. Also, online purchases we make influence the information that comes our way (Bean, 2018).

What can you do to mitigate poor critical thinking since **Bias is All Around You**? Read this book! We will inform you about 7 bias sources of information and the 10 most popular fallacies that can compromise your ability to properly vet all the data you are exposed to each day. You can start to better filter bias and fallacies that can otherwise:

1. Lead you to follow a false cause
2. Leave you feeling foolish
3. Tarnish your credibility
4. Attract the wrong people
5. Create undue stress
6. Compromise your values
7. Harm your mental health

In the end, following information with little or no critical thinking can lead to hostile discussions and perpetuate conspiracy theories. But none of these potentially debilitating results need occur! For it's time to read between the lines and curtail bias now! Together, we can chart a new heartfelt civil discourse, one that uses information more wisely, with prudence and goodwill. So, let's get started.

Sincerely,

Erik Bean

Erik Bean, Ed.D.
July 4th, 2021

Chapter 1. 7 Sources of Bias

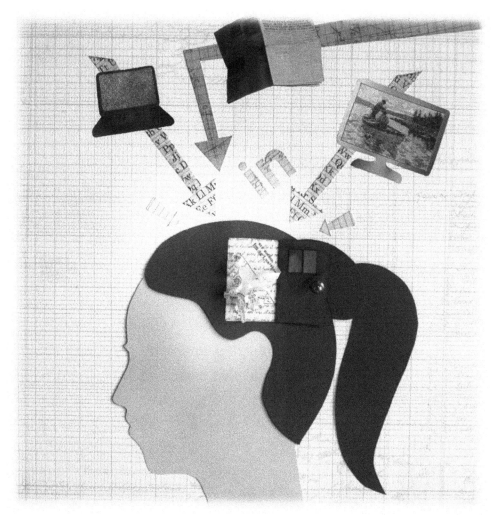

We encounter information via mediums like television and radio programs, newspapers, magazines, books, peer reviewed journals, websites, social media networks, and podcasts. What we absorb influences each of us more deeply than any of us could ever imagine. Each of these published media examples may yield some bias because it is virtually impossible to remove all bias. We all have bias because we all have opinions on everything from how to stop pollution to who should be running our country.

Bias Is All Around You

What is Bias?

According to Dictionary.com (2021), bias is defined as, "a particular tendency, trend, inclination, feeling, or opinion, especially one that is preconceived or unreasoned…" (para 1). Therefore, everyone has bias, and our personal biases are developed from the moment we are born. Such biases are shaped by our family, our faith, our friends, our education, the community that surrounds us, and the media itself (Erikson, 1950; Waszak & Bean, 2019). Our day-to-day challenges and experiences also contribute to our personal biases.

Our biases are so ingrained that we typically shy away from information and people that do not align with our values. While it may not seem as though there are negative consequences to this behavior, it can impede our ability to be objective. Objectivity is defined as striving to seek the truth, being impartial, and staying relevant to humanity in a prudent and positive sense. If we apply critical thinking, we can improve our objectivity.

Before we approach critical thinking, it is important for you to know that each piece of published information that comes our way, whether it is in print, heard on the radio, seen on television, or experienced on the internet should be examined as a single unit that requires screening for any possible bias. To determine the level of bias, we need to analyze how the piece is written and we need to reflect on whether our personal biases impede our ability to objectively assess them. For example, if a piece is written by someone who is a different religion than we are, can we be open to the topic it addresses? If we are a Democrat, can we listen to the advice of a Republican on the economy even if we disagree on other issues? Or vice versa?

Analyzing information, therefore, is a two-way process. You can view the sender as the individual or entity that publishes or otherwise distributes the information and you as the receiver. As the receiver your ability to interpret the information can be impeded by your personal biases and something communication researchers call *semantic noise*. Semantic noise is all the extraneous environmental forces that can interfere with our ability to concentrate (Pickett, 1988).

Examples of semantic noise range from being hungry to trying to multitask. All these semantic noise events also can interfere with our ability to assess bias. Now let's see how we should analyze a piece of information from the get-go.

The First Step in assessing any piece of information is to determine how it was distributed and by whom, for these answers are often tied to an entity and almost every entity has bias because of the values, products, or services it represents. These may not necessarily be negative biases, but it's important to identify the type of bias that holds it accountable to its purpose. In other words, if a piece is designed to provide car buying advice that is bias-free, it should be written by an independent author and should not include a kickback like a gift of a new car for the reviewer. While this example may seem extreme, these situations do occur.

Another area that can affect the way a piece of information is analyzed is the type of data it may contain. For example, if it contains statistics that lead to conclusions, we should examine them carefully. Such statistics should be rigorously analyzed, and if we are going to heed a recommendation, we may want to look for other published information that agrees with it. Bias does not mean material is not useful. It simply means each of us needs to understand where bias can be derived.

Therefore, **Step 2** is to assess the authenticity of the information you are receiving. This refers to the level of transparency of the individual or organization that published it, the date it was published, and the context that derived its purpose. Transparency is the author's ability to be honest about where they obtained their facts and information. When evaluating information decide whether the piece is an editorial, a sales pitch, a peer reviewed research study, scientific fact, or designed to be deceptive.

For example, the book you are reading right now is published by the *Healthy Mind Express* imprint of the Ethan Bean Mental Wellness Foundation, a Michigan 501(c)3 non-profit public charity dedicated to helping people understand mental health issues that many struggling teens and adults suffer from including autism and those who are neurodiverse. Neurodiverse is a term used to describe mental health conditions not readily diagnosable. Established in 2019 following the passing of my 17-year-old son Ethan, the organization focuses on how our hyper-connected internet driven world may lead to isolation and misunderstanding of information among developing young minds and adults.

A portion of the revenue generated from the sale of this book will go to provide programming to help people understand the needs of neurodiverse individuals and provide educational opportunities to help people maintain their mental health. Therefore, no matter what the Ethan Bean Mental Wellness Foundation publishes, that material is designed to uphold its values and purpose.

Bias must be noted to the degree of how it impacts that topic's overall trajectory, the positive or negative message it conveys, and the perception in general people have about it. Finally, the ramifications of the results of distributing the information also should be taken into consideration because writing, speaking, and maintaining a position creates a powerful voice, and for those with a big following, how people react to it can have serious consequences. Therefore, everyone must take the time to discern the overall bias of any information they encounter as it can have a positive or negative impact depending on how they respond to it. The key takeaway is that there are gray areas in bias.

Bias is not inherently a bad thing, but it can tarnish the perception of the information by exaggerating it or understating it if it leaves out important facts that should be discussed. Therefore, **Step 3** is to take your time assessing it. Scrutinizing the level of potential bias, big or small, helps to determine the authenticity of that information, and why it was published. Remember, all information is either tied to organizations or individuals.

Prior to the internet, it was very hard for individuals to contribute to a national conversation. The only way they could possibly have a voice was to submit an editorial to a local newspaper and hope it would get published. However, with the advent of the internet people could take advantage and see their message go viral. Today, individuals can publish their own blogs, post videos, podcasts, and build websites regardless of their backgrounds. But as such, individuals all bring to their materials a certain level of bias. **Step 4** is to employ critical thinking.

Critical Thinking

Critical thinking is a conscious process. Unless you are consciously aware of the need to analyze information for your own physical safety and mental health, you may not be doing so in a productive manner. Therefore, we must be conscious enough to step back, take a deep breath, and think deeply about who created the information, what entity they represent, and whether any hidden agendas are present. Critical thinking is needed to make the process a success. Observing the 7 sources of bias to follow will help you effectively analyze the information no matter where it is found.

Remember, all information has a purpose. We just need to be smarter about identifying the degree of bias that may exist. When we inspect for such bias, we are really *vetting* the material. According to Dictionary.com, vetting means, "to appraise, verify, or check the accuracy, authenticity, validity," (para 3). Once we can properly vet information, then and only then, can we really have an intelligent conversation with colleagues and friends. That said, below are the 7 sources of all potential bias:

1. **Academic**
2. **Hidden Agenda**
3. **For-Profit**
4. **Non-Profit**
5. **Watchdog Groups**
6. **Government**
7. **Individuals**

Bias Is All Around You

1. Academic

The first source is Academic. By this we mean schools, colleges, and universities. This source is on a mission to create knowledge. If we examine higher education, we find that in many cases professors and chairs often need to get published particularly through peer reviewed journals so that their research contributes to the literature in a meaningful way. But this race to get published is often tied to tenure and the money they earn as academicians. As the Ivy League saying goes, "Publish or perish," meaning that a professor cannot earn tenure if the publication does not occur; therefore, he or she might as well perish. For potential bias it could mean they might have overlooked some rigor in their study and that the journal that published it could overlook it too.

We see the scrutiny in such peer reviewed academic research studies all the time. One study says oatmeal is good for us because it is high in fiber. Another says too much oatmeal can lead to too much carbohydrate intake and weight gain. This is not to say either study is false. When screening information derived from higher education, we should examine the schools the research is tied to and the publications the studies are presented in to make sure these are not predatory. Predatory journals are often categorized as publications that require inordinate amount of money for a study to be reviewed or ones that instantly publish a study with little or no rigorous peer review. Therefore, when examining such studies look carefully at the backgrounds of the researchers to determine what, if any, bias exists in their overall effort to lead a conversation in their field. Again, gray areas of bias exist all around us. No study is perfect.

2. Hidden Agenda Groups

Hidden Agenda Groups purport to represent one or several causes, but covertly may represent one or several nefarious undertakings. The information they distribute may be hard to track to a single person or agency. They also may be hard to contact since they really are not in the business of being transparent. Nor do they provide accurate information.

Bias Is All Around You

Groups like QAnon who magnify and circulate conspiracy theories are identified as a hidden agenda group. QAnon also recruits prominent people in power who might use the information to amplify their messages, to further their own hidden agendas, to enhance their political standing, or to simply bolster their careers (Kuznia, et. al., 2020). Some of these entities are found in the form of apps, or dangerous computer code masquerading as a friendly game, or a website whose users were drawn there by misleading search engine descriptions.

More recently, TikTok, the popular video sharing application, was accused of allegedly collecting and distributing user data for political or other possible nefarious purposes (McMillan, et. al., 2020). Applications have less impactful hidden agendas that may include buying or selling user data. For example, Facebook, Google, and LinkedIn, have been accused of violating user privacy policies. In Facebook's case, a company known as Cambridge Analytics knowingly used the social media giant's database of users for their own hidden agenda purposes.

"As Facebook reeled, The New York Times delved into the relationship between Cambridge Analytica and John Bolton, the conservative hawk named national security adviser by President Trump. The Times broke the news that in 2014, Cambridge provided Mr. Bolton's "super PAC" with early versions of its Facebook-derived profiles — the technology's first large-scale use in an American election" (Confessore, 2018, para 9).

Quite simply put, you may not ever be able to judge the bias in these groups' materials because their materials are designed to be deceptive like propaganda. They may look like a game or a traditional website that portrays that they represent a good cause but underneath they are funneling data or revenue for another purpose. In sum, we need to be aware that hidden agendas and hidden agenda groups are out there. In a worst-case scenario, if we accidentally paraphrase or quote them, we may be perpetuating their self-interests as our own.

3. For-Profit

The third source is For-Profit. For-Profit organizations represent most of the information we are exposed to because our culture is primarily fashioned upon a free enterprise market system. The goal of for-profit organizations is to influence you to purchase their product. Therefore, bias is inherent in their sales techniques. Ford Motor Company is one example.

Ford is in the business of manufacturing cars. When Ford advertises their products, obviously their goal is to get people interested in buying them. But like all companies, they are subject to truth in advertising. They can make claims that are independently verified but should not exaggerate such claims just to make a profit. Throughout the years many automobile manufacturers both domestic and international have been caught exaggerating claims from performance, to gas mileage, to air emission ratings (Brown, 2018). As such, many for-profit companies try to appeal to your emotions and overvalue their product to make sales. Therefore, double check other sources like Consumer Reports.

4. Non-Profit

Non-Profits are either public charities, philanthropic foundations, or an enterprise that serves industry or education. Examples include churches and temples, governments, some business associations, municipalities, and other community enterprises. The Young Men's Christian Association (YMCA), American Foundation for Suicide Prevention, the American Marketing Association, and the United Negro College Fund, have been reliable examples of popular non-profits. It is important to vet all publicized information pertaining to non-profits by carefully examining any claims they make about where funds are distributed and if their actions align with the values they publicize.

5. Watchdog Groups

The purpose of watchdog groups is to monitor other groups by employing a checks and balances approach. They measure the value these groups hold for humanity. For example, People for the Ethical Treatment of Animals (PETA) helps spread awareness about animal safety and wellbeing and others like the Gun Violence Archive (GVA) track incidents

of gun violence across America. Others track water resources such as the Environmental Working Group (Bote, 2020). Watchdog groups may contain any number of biases or hidden agendas as well that could possibly lead people to follow a false cause if they are not authentic or transparent in their published communications. Most watchdog groups are organized as non-profits and provide a philanthropic approach to their public value. Like any nonprofit scrutinize watchdogs to be sure they are legitimate.

6. Government

Government entities are many. In the United States there are numerous agencies and departments. From the United States Department of Agriculture (USDA) to the Centers for Disease Control and Prevention (CDC) to the White House, there are literally dozens upon dozens of governmental units, and each publishes mounds of reports, demographics, advisories, studies, research, and warnings (USA.gov). Bias within these reports might be tied to lobbyists or legislation that is profitable to certain other entities or contain "pork."

Pork is extra initiatives and/or funding that typically has nothing to do with a bill's real purpose. For example, a bill designed to provide homeowners with tax relief in a certain geographic area, may also fund other out of state projects.

Therefore, we must inspect underlying forces that require the bill to be created. The same holds true for many government reports. We should ask ourselves how were they funded, and what purpose do they ultimately serve? The statistical data often associated with such reports is vulnerable to manipulation. Mark Twain (Samuel Clemens) said more than 100 years ago, "Figures don't lie, but liars figure."

Government reports should be rigorous in terms of sample size and proper research method application. So, when assessing these reports pay careful attention to possible bias associated with the politics behind the governmental unit itself. Were these reports influenced by other agencies or people who may have censored some of the information after or prior to its release?

Governmental agency reports are sometimes produced to enhance their own hidden agendas. They can generate reports they do not want the public to even know about. Jesse Ventura, a former independent governor of Minnesota, wrote about these reports in his co-authored Simon & Schuster book, *63 Documents the Government Doesn't Want You to Read* (Ventura & Russell, 2021). However, in other instances, the government has a right to keep secrets such as nuclear codes, military plans, and those in the best interest of national security.

Therefore, it is important to rigorously review the data you receive. When vetting these kinds of reports, closely examine the legislation that might have originally been created to yield the governmental studies and laws. Do these reports reflect more facts rather than opinion? For example, according to a Washington Post investigative piece, U.S. officials misled the public about the War in Afghanistan for many years via a variety of government documents the paper obtained (Whitlock, 2019).

As a precaution for any of the bias sources assessed, be sure you download or examine the data from the original source that published it if possible. For if you do not obtain it from the original source, you run the risk that the data was reinterpreted differently than it was meant.

Remember that children's game *Operator* played sitting down in a big circle? One child would whisper a piece of information and by the time it came full circle, it was often distorted from its original meaning. Likewise, information that we receive from the media and social networks may have been transformed from its original meaning by the time we receive it. Sifting for less biased information works best by obtaining that information from its original source.

7. Individuals

Individuals are categorized into their own group simply because they can publish, share, and distribute information that they or others create. Independence lends itself to personal bias overtly or covertly tied to a hidden agenda. The only way to fairly assess any level of individual bias is to evaluate the background or character of the writer or speaker.

Now that we have covered the 7 sources of potential bias, we can explore different ways to separate facts from fiction. To use information wisely, we must vet it for accuracy and objectivity. One of the most powerful tools is to examine the rhetorical style that comprises the piece. I created a method that takes all the rhetorical styles into consideration and allows you to start assessing levels of accuracy and inherent bias that I dub KLEMP.

KLEMP Test

KLEMP is an acronym for Kairos, Logos, Ethos, Mythos, and Pathos. Kairos refers to the immediacy and timeliness of the information when it was published. Logos means statistics or facts. Ethos and mythos are rhetorical styles that have a somewhat similar meaning. Ethos is the background or character of the writer. It refers to the qualifications of the writer or speaker. To know whether the background of the writer's work has directly inspired his or her thought process for any given published piece, it's important to do a little investigating. Ethos is not inherently a negative relationship. In many cases the author's background enriches his or her work, particularly in the creative fields of music, fiction, poetry, and film making.

For example, Steven Spielberg is Jewish. He had family members in the Holocaust. He directed and produced the award winning 1993 movie *Schindler's List*. Spielberg's ethos was fundamental to creating a film that resonated with people from many religious sects. His attention to detail enabled him to connect with his audience.

Mythos is like ethos, but instead of being built upon the writer's entire background, it is an ongoing set of assumptions, values, or beliefs about a particular field of study, or specific issue. Mythos also can represent what he or she frequently publishes, which is known as their Subject Matter Expertise (SME). We can generally view a subject matter expert as someone who contributes to their field or the subject of discussion for the good of humanity. But if someone frequently publishes pieces with hatred or prejudicial values, their SME should become null and void. For purposes of assessing mythos, we would recommend scoring mythos a 5 or high in bias as shown in the **Bias Assessment Form** found in the Appendix. The final style is pathos which means emotion (Montgomery College, n.d.). Now that you know what KLEMP is, we can use it to assess the literary style.

Assessing Literary Style

When you receive a piece of information put KLEMP into action. Start with kairos to evaluate when the information was published. Is there a date? Was it published within the last day, week, or month? Older published pieces are not necessarily a negative attribute, but can be if newer data, facts, or statistics are available.

Next, examine logos to determine the number of facts, statistics, and citations it may contain. Information that is rigorous should include one or more reputable other sources of data or facts. If the information is void of other sources it is said to be idiosyncratic in its scope, the equivalent of an editorial. Well documented pieces of information are inherently more authentic and objective.

Now it is time to investigate ethos and mythos to understand the writer's beliefs, value system, and level of knowledge. For ethos, open an internet search engine and search the author using their published name. What does the search reveal about his or her background, upbringing, hurdles he or she may have overcome? Many authors use their background to contribute positively to humanity, but some can get so caught up in their own agendas that a published piece might provide too much of the author's own bias to be objective. If you believe this to be true, the published piece may contain some bias associated with ethos. But this can be difficult to ascertain, and it also depends on how well your personal values and own biases align with it.

For mythos, the analysis is not just on the author's background, but on what is believed to be his or her Subject Matter Expertise (SME). This is based on what he or she most frequently writes about. If you can identify more than three published pieces on the same subject by the same author, mythos might be established. Be aware that mythos can be a positive attribute, or negative one if someone is frequently spewing hatred or otherwise not contributing positively to humanity. In general, a negative mythos analysis may be accompanied by a hidden agenda.

Finally, we must assess the piece for pathos. Is the piece simply emotionally driven or void of logos (facts)? Does the piece include other sources?

Now it is time to apply KLEMP. You can apply all five assessments in order. However, if your time is limited, I suggest you begin with kairos, logos, and pathos only. If you include ethos and mythos right away it will require an internet search. The following examples use only kairos, logos, and pathos which can provide the fastest insight to assess if a piece looks bias.

Less Bias

kairos, logos, and *pathos* = timely, data driven, little emotion

More Bias

kairos, pathos, and *logos* = timely, emotionally driven, some or no data

Bias Is All Around You

Heavy Bias

pathos, logos, and *kairos* = emotionally driven, some data, not timely

If the piece contains no documented facts at all, the order might look like:

Extreme Bias

pathos and *kairos* = emotionally driven only and not timely (typically even more bias regardless of the topic)

If you assess a piece like the one above, think very carefully if your values align with it. Is it worth sharing in a social network or would you be perpetuating a false narrative? Do your due diligence and take the author's name and run it through a search engine. Your detective work may ask:

1. What possible bias source does the individual or entity represent?
2. What causes might they support?
3. Are there other examples of divisive postings or other published pieces that might be cause for alarm?
4. Is there any direct conflict of interests between the purpose of the publication and its author or speaker?
5. Which KLEMP style is more prominent than the others?

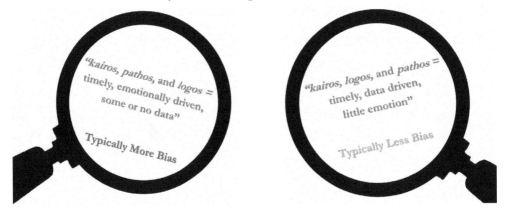

Do you have to do the entire KLEMP test with every piece of published information? Not necessarily. But you do have to do this if the information is controversial or could lead to disenfranchising your network as well as your close friends, particularly if you assume the position of any person or entity.

Vet to Avert Fallacies

Inspecting information is not complete until it is vetted for fallacies. In its simplest form a fallacy is a misbelief or erroneous piece of information with no attribution or verification. Over the centuries, fallacies have been broken down into certain categories. We will discuss these in Chapter 6. But until we get there, if you are going to share any information be sure it is current or let your network know the publication date and the context in which the information was published. This will reflect that you are transparent and allows the receiver to easily vet the material. Remember, as you look at any published piece of information, or listen to an audio clip, or watch a video, first determine which of the 7 sources of potential bias it can be categorized as and then employ these first four steps:

Step 1): Determine how it was distributed and by whom.

Step 2): Assess the authenticity and objectivity of the information.

Step 3): Take your time.

Step 4): Employ critical thinking.

Now let's see what's at stake if we do not properly apply critical thinking.

Bias Is All Around You

Chapter 2. Disregarding Bias for Mental Health

Not long ago we received our news by watching television, listening to the radio, or buying a newspaper. We automatically took more time to vet information because we spent more time finding it. Because there were fewer choices our news sources were more reliable. Today, however, some of the traditional news networks have sided with politics or catered to advertising dollars.

To complicate matters, according to Broussard, Diakopoulos, Guzman, Abebe, Dupagne, and Chuan (2019), information we search for on the internet is typically part of a cavalcade of algorithms that can be bought to influence a particular audience via news, products, or services. Thus, since information can be bought and manipulated through algorithms, it influences what we may be exposed to via searches and online shopping. We are exposed to a seemingly never-ending blitz of competing data that pummels our smartphones, search engines, and laptop computers.

Algorithms, Helpful or Harmful?

An algorithm is a computer program that is designed to filter, concentrate, or manipulate digital information for any number of purposes. An algorithm can be helpful to track your heart rate via your smartwatch or it can analyze what you like to purchase and serve you up similar items for faster searching. But algorithms can also potentially harm us by controlling the news we are exposed to or the social media posts we most frequently see (Broussard, et. al., 2019).

Such algorithms could lead to fake news or ads that masquerade as news (Bean, 2018). The ads themselves may be fake and may not offer what they appear to promise. They may also be used to gather your personal information. By employing all the assessment methods we discussed, hopefully you can stave off these annoying pieces of information and not become a victim to their less than authentic message.

That said, no one wants to be recklessly manipulated by information delivered to them by an algorithm, but we must all strive to do a better job at reading between the bias algorithm lines. What's at stake? Our future value system as we know it. Not properly analyzing information can:

1. Lead you to follow a false cause

2. Leave you feeling foolish

3. Tarnish your credibility

4. Attract the wrong people

5. Create undue stress

6. Compromise your values

7. Harm your mental health

Joseph Pulitzer, Legacy of a New York Congressman and Non-Bias Purveyor of News

This unabashed disregard for truth propagated in many social networks (one of the biggest misinformation data aggregates) has resulted in political and global economic strife the likes of which have not been experienced since the printing press was invented over 500 years ago. In 1904 Pulitzer wrote, **"Our Republic and its press will rise or fall together..."** (Topping, 2018, para 22).

If we choose to recklessly share information without vetting, much is at stake personally as well as politically. If we fall victim to any of the 10 fallacies we will soon discuss, our mental health may be comprised! We may experience what psychologists call cognitive dissonance, an uncomfortable psychological state that exists when there are inconsistencies between one's behaviors and cognitions (Festinger, 1957).

Such cognitive dissonance can cause much emotional pain and physical hardship leading to negative, stressful consequences (Migliore & Bean, 2020). The simplest example of cognitive dissonance can represent the feeling someone

experiences after eating a meal they knew was unhealthy. Can someone experience such cognitive dissonance from how they absorb or share information? Only you can answer that question. But there is an ethical line that can be broken if we share information without thoroughly inspecting it. This may circulate a false narrative.

But there is good news. If we choose authenticity by seeking the truth or vetting what may likely be false, then this type of reconnaissance may safeguard our mental health and allow us to think objectively. Chapter 3 will show you that when you are willing to be objective and critically think about information, you can embrace the information you have gathered more confidently.

Chapter 3. Good News!

Indeed, there are more than enough sources of information within media outlets to have checks and balances. From newspapers to television and radio networks, most journalism entities have covered news with a non-bias mirrored approach. The idea that such news outlets are liberal came from reporting the facts to mirror them. Therefore, many older newspapers contained the word *mirror* in their name. They were dedicated to mirroring the news, not sensationalizing it.

More recently, the terms *liberal* and *mainstream* for that matter have been exaggerated and sensationalized. Some on the far right have charged the liberal mainstream media with perpetuating deep liberal policies that align with socialism. But the mainstream press overall has done a good job using their trained journalistic personnel and have stuck to their mirroring pledge. In fact, according to the *Oxford Language Dictionary*, the definition of liberal means, "willing to respect or accept behavior or opinions different from one's own; open to new ideas," (para 1). For trained journalists, that means they strive to remain neutral. They report the news and attempt to clarify the events without blending in editorials. This is not to say that some newspapers and television networks can't lean towards the right or left depending on their ownership.

Outliers

Luckily, other tools are available to debunk news bias including examining outliers. Outliers are documented trails of evidence that help balance facts from fiction. For example, we can obtain original courtroom filings, we can read complete court verdicts, and we can acquire meeting minutes from our local municipalities to find out who said what and under what pretext. We can closely examine the language in laws by obtaining the actual law again from a municipality or using library database searches.

We strive to accept the known facts first to avoid hasty generalizations and we should strive to reject conspiracy theories that often will never have enough evidence decades from now to hold true. It is true that for some events it can take years or decades to learn the truth, but those who perpetuate false narratives today without acknowledging they can be wrong are not maintaining civil discourse. As Reader (2012) noted, civility means polite in terms of discourse. Uncivil people sow mistrust and can anger those susceptible to manipulation. Only known processes and facts can be legitimately and openly debated.

Therefore, never solely rely on one source, whether a social network or well-known news outlet, for all your news. If you believe you have been a victim of fake news or were led to believe a false cause, you are not alone. It can happen to anyone, those highly educated or those who never set foot in school.

So stand by for Chapter 4 as we provide 6 Tests to Judge Reliable Journalistic Sources. Then later in Chapter 5 we will further emphasize how to avoid hasty generalizations that affect our mental health as well as our reputation among our peers.

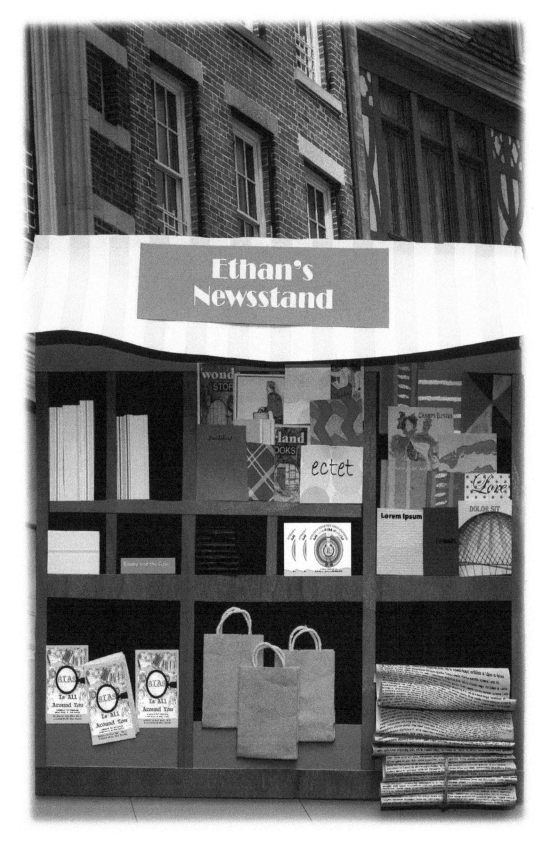

Chapter 4. How to Test Journalistic Sources

Some sources of information are categorized as journalistic. Prior to the internet, the traditional news mediums were the only sources of official news other than independent magazines and association newsletters. The various news agencies decided based on their own arbitrary analysis of stories which ones should be publicly released. Thus, they were known as the gatekeepers of the news. Much has been studied about how such journalistic operations prioritize news releases and how prominently they cover such stories (Shoemaker & Vos, 2009). Then, as today, we hope they rigorously take a non-bias approach to accuracy in their stories. But all news must be assessed and vetted for their ownership can frequently change hands or side with politics or be tied to funding or other conflicts of interest. Therefore, these 6 tests can help discern any gray areas of bias that might otherwise affect the authenticity of their work:

1. Is the source under scrutiny a reliable one? Has it existed for many years? Is its agenda hidden?

2. Do their views appear to be freely expressed regardless of the financial support they receive?

    For example, a national news network like NBC reports on a controversial issue associated with the entity Peloton (an exercise bike company) it owns (Stump, 2019). We question, can such a conflict of interest affect the rigor of the reporting?

3. Does this journalistic source represent the best in journalistic training? Do they employ people who have been professionally trained as a reporter? Do they maintain neutrality and mirror the news, not editorialize it?

4. Does the source suppress sensationalism known as *yellow journalism*? Tabloids employ yellow journalism by dramatizing and exaggerating to capture their audience.

5. Is the source searchable in a library database?

6. Do such outlets typically take on a one-sided political view?

Be mindful, as of late 2020 six corporations, Comcast, NBCUniversal, Disney, CBS, Viacom News Corporation, and AT&T, control approximately 90 percent of all media outlets in America (Louise, 2020). Objectivity and some bias can be present in any of these news divisions and their subsidiaries.

The above tests help to discern gray areas and levels of bias that can affect the authenticity of published pieces. These tests should be applied to avoid hasty generalization in sharing information, whether it was propagated from an individual or any of the entities within the 7 bias sources. Be aware that quantity of postings or claims does not substantiate news. Quality of the claims, who represents them, under what bias sources they are made, and whether such claims are already vetted by many are keys to contributing to everyday successful informational analysis.

Chapter 5. Hasty Generalizations: Reinforcing Reliability Tests!

We assess information for reliability. We do this to discover any bias associated with it before we share it in our social networks or include it in an essay, report, or any information we make public. We use all the reliability tests at our disposal primarily to avoid being a victim of a hasty generalization. So remember to:

Bias Is All Around You

1. Examine when the information was published and by whom.

2. Identify what biases the source may overtly and covertly represent.

3. Vet any piece of textual, audio, or video information tied to each of the *7 Sources of Bias* using the 4 steps outlined in Chapter 1 as well as those referred to in KLEMP.

If we immediately share the information without using all the reliability tests available, we may commit a Hasty Generalization. It is easy to impulsively use information to validate that we are right but then we risk compromising our values and endangering our mental health as well as the mental health of others. We may share something that simply is not true.

Sharing sensationalized or ill-conceived information is a dangerous affair and impedes one's credibility over time. Note that in 2018 the Oxford Internet Institute revealed some people shared information in their social networks without vetting it just to help get a political candidate elected, or they did vet it and knew the information was not legitimate but seemed harmless to share (Oxford Internet Institute, 2018).

Chapter 6. Understanding Fallacies

We can either accidentally be a victim of a fallacy or we can inadvertently promote one. According to Dictionary.com (2021), a fallacy is, "a deceptive, misleading, or false notion, belief, etc.: *That the world is flat was at one time a popular fallacy*" (para 1). These are the 10 most prominent fallacies. Being aware of these fallacies will enable you to maintain your authenticity and to better scrutinize the authenticity of others.

1. **Ad Hominen:** Attacking an opponent.
2. **Ad Populum**: Many people believe it is true, but it might not be true. Also known as Jumping on the Band Wagon.
3. **Appeal to Authority:** Someone in power says they are right, but they may be wrong.
4. **Begging the Question**: Author's premise and conclusion are identical.
5. **False Dichotomy:** Only showing two possible conclusions when there are more.
6. **Hasty Generalization**: Lack of critical thinking and lack of properly vetted information leads to immediately believing.

7. **Post Hoc/False Cause:** Overgeneralization. For example, if an event predicts another event, it must have also caused that event.
8. **Missing the Point** (also known as Red Herring): A speaker makes a conclusion but not one related to the argument.
9. **Spotlight Fallacy:** A subject that gets much publicity but may be overgeneralized drawing attention from the important facts. The heightened publicity takes away from the real issue at hand.
10. **Straw Man:** An author puts forward an opponent's weaker, less critical issue to overshadow the real situation that is occurring. (International Institute of Debate, 2016).

As you critically read through any piece of information, be sure to examine whether you believe it contains any fallacies. Analyzing such information is a qualitative process and can best be accomplished when you first think about your own biases. Do your biases impede your ability to be objective in your analysis? It can be easy to say a piece contains a fallacy if you do not like the author for no reason other than their views differ from yours.

Let us define these fallacies further to see how we must curtail their damaging consequences to rational critical thinking. Understand that in most cases the piece itself can have any of these fallacies embedded in it. But based on your personal biases, you might perpetuate a fallacy like hasty generalization if you do not take the time to analyze it.

1. **Ad Hominen:** Attacking an opponent.

This fallacy is related to prejudice. In this scenario we do not like someone. Therefore, no matter what they say, we choose not to listen and simply attack them. For example, if you are a Republican, you may ignore a Democrat. Likewise, if you are Democrat, you may ignore a Republican's opposing belief. Prejudice is not just about religion or gender. Ad Hominen can be at play. While assessing the piece use your best judgement to discern whether it contains Ad Hominen and conversely ask yourself if your personal biases perpetuate this fallacy to the point where you cannot be amenable to absorbing the message if it is logically argued and if it is timely.

2. **Ad Populum**: Many people believe something is true, but it might not be true. Also, known as Jumping on the Band Wagon.

Many believe this fallacy was well at work throughout the 2020 U.S. election. But should we believe the election was rigged simply because people repeatedly said that it was, or do we have other outlying information on which to base this idea? Frequency does not necessarily equal truth. Popularity does not necessarily equal the truth. If you Jump on the Bandwagon, do your research first. All elections have some acceptable margin of error. Do such pieces contain reliable facts and attribution? Are such published pieces fair in their analysis?

3. **Appeal to Authority:** Someone in power says they are right, but they may be wrong.

Dr. Anthony Fauci is the U.S. authority on infectious diseases and has served six Republican and Democratic presidential cabinets. What he says about disease, how it spreads, and how it can be avoided should be heeded. In my analysis of several pieces in the spring of 2021, I determined that Dr. Fauci's kairos reflects the use of current data, his logos demonstrates it is backed by statistics and facts, his ethos refers to 40 years of medical experience in a leadership role, and his mythos has been safeguarding citizens. Lastly, his pathos displays a passion for helping others.

However, some people in power can mislead their followers. In many cases the authorities that serve us do so with authenticity to earnestly help us. But throughout history we have seen many in authority abuse their authenticity and power, and make false claims for personal, political, financial, academic, or corporate benefit.

We may see corruption within any of the 7 published bias sources. Is the piece written by someone who has compromised their power and possibly abused it? Are you able to assess the piece by an authority figure who you believe is authentic? Do they provide attribution within their published texts or speeches that is validated by several sources?

4. **Begging the Question**: Author's premise and conclusion are identical.

Here an individual or entity asks readers, consumers, or followers to simply believe them. People who beg the question want you to implicitly trust them. We can say that most parents are purveyors of Begging the Question a million times a day. Parents want their children to accept their advice or instruction as true. Children may ask, "why?" Parents may respond erroneously, "because I said so!" Parents are trying to work in the best interest of their children. But others such as corporate or non-profit leaders, and politicians, for example, with possible hidden agendas also want you to believe them; however, like parents, they may not be prepared to defend their claims. It is one thing to make a claim. It is another thing to defend it with evidence and proof.

5. **False Dichotomy:** Only showing two possible conclusions when there are more.

It has been said, "There are two sides to every story." However, this edict that has been propagated for decades is not necessarily so. There can be three, four, five, or ten sides to a story. If we were not there, we cannot say with certainty what happened.

Best to avoid false dichotomy since this premise only contains two possible outcomes when many may lie below the surface. While vetting, consider does the piece only look at one or two sides? How many sides are possible? In some small instances there might only be two positions, but often other perspectives exist. Let data (logos) and attribution (citations) be your guide as well as critical thinking and becoming well read on the topic. Sometimes, we think we are an expert on a topic, but until you have read many sides and gotten your hands on much published information, you can become a victim of this fallacy.

6. **Hasty Generalization**: Lack of critical thinking and lack of properly screening information.

This is the most abused fallacy which is why we dedicated Chapter 5 to it.

7. **Post Hoc/False Cause:** Overgeneralization. If one event predicts another event, it must have also triggered that event.

For example, just because you have a friend from Boston known for its delicious seafood, this does not mean when your friend comes over for dinner, they will want lobster.

8. **Missing the Point** (also known as Red Herring): a speaker makes a conclusion but not one related to the argument.

This is akin to a bait and switch. A conclusion is drawn but does not relate to the discussion. According to The Happy Neuron, a WordPress watchdog group, "Listen to Trump speak for 30 seconds and he will use a red herring fallacy. The most recent example of this happened during Trump's Mt. Rushmore speech, in which he miscategorized the protests and riots sparked by the murder of George Floyd as a 'merciless campaign to wipe out our history.' While it's true that monuments are being taken down, he is not addressing the real issue here: institutional racism and police brutality" (The Happy Neuron, 2020, para 17). Are you able to analyze a piece for not only what it states, but what it infers? You need to do so to avert this fallacy.

9. **Spotlight Fallacy:** A subject that gets much publicity but may be overgeneralized drawing attention away from the important facts.

Like Post Hoc/False Cause, but the Spotlight Fallacy refers to a topic that gets the most publicity or news coverage. This gives the illusion it is most important.

10. **Straw Man:** Author puts forward an opponent's weaker, less critical issue to overshadow the real situation that is occurring (International Institute of Debate, 2016).

Former 45th United States President Donald Trump is a master of the straw man fallacy! He often focuses on a superficial weakness of his opponents so his followers will only focus on frivolous shortcomings, not the real political issues at stake. In addition, his rhetoric has painted the "liberal" media as the enemy of the people. "The FAKE NEWS media (failing @nytimes, @NBCNews, @ABC, @CBS, @CNN) is not my enemy, it is the enemy of the American People!"(Meeks, 2020, para 2). Is the person attacking another individual?

When assessing any piece of information, you should strive to not let that piece of information outsmart you. Instead, be wise and properly vet it for any fallacies it might contain and employ your best critical thinking and detective work to understand the biases that might be associated with it. For fallacies, the **Bias Assessment Form** located in the Appendix offers a scale to rate the piece from 1 to 5. A rating of 1 means that no fallacies likely exist. A rating of 5 means any one or more of the 10 fallacies discussed are prominent. You can download a new form if you wish for every document you analyze at our website BiasHandbook.com/tools. The PDF file is password protected. Please enter: **Mybiasbook2024** to access. Let's summarize how important proper vetting is for our own mental health and in helping to maintain civil discourse in Chapter 7.

Chapter 7. Summary:
A Renewed Call for Civil Discourse

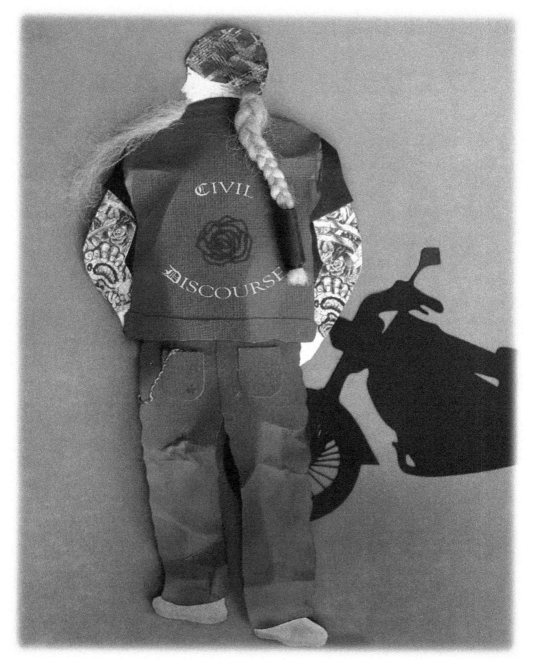

Bias Is All Around You

We've entered a crisis in civil discourse, one we have never seen before. Where is the leadership to help the public understand bias? Does it lie only with the journalism profession or can leaders from many industries and academia help people take the time needed to critically think and properly investigate conflicting information? Improperly vetting information has become a prominent mental health issue of this decade that can lead to mental fatigue. In its simplest form it can cause stress and at its worst it can elicit overwhelming feelings of anger, guilt, fear, and hopelessness. This can lead individuals to harm themselves or others and the results can be fatal.

The crisis didn't necessarily begin in the west, but the west fueled it in so many ways. The American social network giants whose unabashed use of aggressive algorithms and distribution of fake news for a profit centric model led some affiliates, and millions of subscribers, into an unvetted swamp of disinformation. In some cases, the fake news was further hijacked by hidden agenda groups with destructive ideologies. They spread hatred which was supported by politicians who were seeking votes.

The 2020 U.S. presidential election, civil unrest, the pandemic, and a crushing global economy also fueled a waning public discourse from civil to rude. Second, many in the public grew accustomed to reading filtered news from search engines like Google and Microsoft's Bing. They may have confused frequency of news items with the truth. Finally, some people shared information just to get their candidate of choice elected (Oxford Internet Institute, 2018). They allowed their biases to dictate their decision and ignored the vetting process. The result contributed to many hateful uprisings that shattered and ended lives by those who followed false causes.

Some traditional news networks' own political bias further eroded the public's faith already bruised by years of political mistrust since the 1950s McCarthy era and efforts to track terrorism when the George W. Bush Administration set into place the Patriot Act and the Obama Administration extended it. The Act allows the U.S. government to continue eavesdropping on citizens for any reason, not just those who might be prone to partake in a domestic or international terrorism act.

Other examples that have eroded the mistrust in government include the once ongoing Afghanistan conflict. U.S. officials misled the public about the War in Afghanistan for many years (Whitlock, 2019). It's no wonder the 2020s have created the perfect storm of civil unrest and uncivil discourse. However, much of it is due to a lack of public understanding about bias. Much of the unabashed disregard for truth propagated in many social networks has resulted in unprecedented political and global strife not experienced since the printing press was invented 500 years ago.

If the public chooses to recklessly share unauthenticated information much is at stake personally, including the freedoms we now enjoy. If people fall victim to any of the commonly known fallacies tied to poor bias vetting, their mental health can continue to be comprised. They may experience what psychologists call cognitive dissonance (Festinger, 1957). This mental health condition is an uncomfortable psychological state that exists when there are inconsistencies between one's behaviors and cognitions. For example, if you share a piece of information that you know is a false narrative you risk compromising your own integrity. This can result in much emotional pain and physical hardship leading to negative, stressful consequences.

Fortunately, we can avoid cognitive dissonance. If the public understands how the information they experience can be manipulated by algorithms, and if they can take the time to properly inspect information, then civil discourse stands a chance at surviving an otherwise tumultuous period in technology, corporate greed, and the battle to squash a worldwide pandemic. The goal is to help the public move towards virtuous leadership (Wang & Hackett, 2020).

Recently, there has been a renewed interest in virtuous leadership. According to Hendriks, et. al. (2020), "virtuous leadership is defined here on a global level as a leadership style where the leader's voluntary (i.e. intrinsically motivated and intentional) behavior consistently exhibited in context-relevant situations aligns with the virtues of prudence, temperance, humanity, courage, and justice" (p. 955, para 1). The use of virtuous leadership to help people understand how to vet bias information is a skill we should all strive to utilize and promote.

Here people can strive to lesson cognitive dissonance so they can choose more wisely before sharing unvetted discourse, curtail following false causes and keep mental health in check. Under a nation driven by free speech there are penalties for falsely screaming fire in a theater. We should all ask ourselves even with the truth vetted, why would some people still want to share a false narrative? After all, we are all part of the disinformation problem in some form, and we should all strive to curtail it. Always inspect information because bias is all around you. Vet information using the 7 major sources of bias. Use critical thinking, avoid hasty generalization, employ the KLEMP tests of rhetorical style and screen for obvious fallacies. Ask yourself, do my personal biases prevent me from accepting the facts or rejecting what might be a false narrative? All the best as you strive to vet bias for your mental health, the stability of our communities and overall success!

"Under a nation driven by free speech there are penalties for falsely screaming fire in a theater. We should all ask ourselves even with the truth vetted, why would some people still want to share a false narrative?"

References

Bean. E. (2018). Industrial age advertising identity solutions for a 21st century social network driven world. Internet, Politics, Policy 2018: Long Live Democracy. Oxford Internet Institute, St. Anne's College, Oxford University, Sept 21, 2018.

Bote, J. (2020). Toxic 'forever chemicals' found in drinking water throughout US. https://www.usatoday.com/story/news/health/2020/01/23/pfas-toxic-forever-chemicals-found-drinking-water-throughout-us/4540909002/

Broussard, M., Diakopoulos, N., Guzman, A. L., Abebe, R., Dupagne, M., & Chuan, C.-H. (2019). Artificial intelligence and journalism. *Journalism & Mass Communication Quarterly, 96*(3), 673–695.

Brown, N. (2018). 20 car ads that totally lied to us. https://www.hotcars.com/20-car-ads-that-totally-lied-to-us/

Confessore, N. (2018). Cambridge Analytica and Facebook: The scandal and fallout so far. https://www.nytimes.com/2018/04/04/us/politics/cambridge-analytica-scandal-fallout.html

Dictionary.com (2021). Bias. https://www.dictionary.com/browse/bias?s=t

Dictionary.com (2021). Vetting. Retrieved from https://www.dictionary.com/browse/vetting?s=t

Erikson, E. (1950). Childhood and society. New York, NY: Norton.

Festinger, L. (1957). *The theory of cognitive dissonance.* Stanford, CA; Stanford University Press.

Hammel, P. (2020). Watchdog group files complaint against Nebraska treasurer, who says charge is without merit. https://omaha.com/state-and-regional/watchdog-group-files-complaint-against-nebraska-treasurer-who-says-charge-is-without-merit/article_c47a64c5-e39c-5bb8-97f9-36ce035f7c5d.html

International Institute of Debate (2016). 10 common logical fallacies. Retrieved from http://iidebate.org/10-common-logical-fallacies/

Joyella, M. (2021). Former CPAC chair tells CNN's Erin Burnett the GOP is now, 'a cult.' https://www.forbes.com/sites/markjoyella/2021/02/26/former-cpac-chair-tells-cnns-erin-burnett-the-gop-is-now-a-cult/?sh=f6e717656f7c

Kuznia, R, Devine, C., & Griffin, D. (2020). How QAnon's lies are hijacking the national conversation. https://www.cnn.com/2020/12/15/us/qanon-trump-twitter-invs/index.html

Louise, N. (2020). These 6 corporations control 90% of the media outlets in America. The illusion of choice and objectivity. https://techstartups.com/2020/09/18/6-corporations-control-90-media-america-illusion-choice-objectivity-2020/

McMillan, R., Lin, L., & Li, S. (2020). TikTok user data: What does the app collect and why are U.S. authorities concerned? https://www.wsj.com/articles/tiktok-user-data-what-does-the-app-collect-and-why-are-u-s-authorities-concerned-11594157084

Migliore, L.A. & Bean, E. (2020). *20/20 Prudent leadership: Values.* Abundant Knowledge, L.L.C.

MEEKS, L. Defining the enemy: How Donald Trump frames the news media. *Journalism & Mass Communication Quarterly*, [s. l.], v. 97, n. 1, p. 211–234, 2020.

Montgomery College. (n.d.). Rhetoric rhetorical appeals. https://www.montgomerycollege.edu/_documents/academics/support/learning-centers/writing-reading-learning-ctr-rockville/student-resources-tech/rhetorical-appeals.pdf

Oxford Internet Institute. (2018). Polarization, partnership and junk news consumption on social media during the 2018 US midterm elections. https://comprop.oii.ox.ac.uk/research/posts/polarization-partisanship-and-junk-news-consumption-on-social-media-during-the-2018-us midterm-elections/#continue

Oxford Language Dictionary. (2021). Liberal. https://www.oxfordlearnersdictionaries.com/us/definition/english/liberal_2

Pickett, J. (1988). SEMANTIC NOISE AND THE CLASSROOM. *ETC: A Review of General Semantics, 45*(3), 278-280. http://www.jstor.org/stable/42582024

Reader, B. (2012). Free press vs. Free speech? The rhetoric of "Civility" in regard to anonymous online comments. *Journalism & Mass Communication* Quarterly, *89*(3), 495–513.

Shoemaker, P.J., & Vos, T.P. (2009). *Gatekeeping theory.* Routledge; Taylor & Francis Group.

Stump, S. (2019). Peloton responds to backlash over holiday commercial, says it was 'misinterpreted.' https://www.today.com/news/peloton-faces-backlash-ridicule-over-new-holiday-commercial-t169080

The Happy Neuron. (2020). How Trump buried the national debate with logical fallacies. http://thehappyneuron.com/2020/07/how-trump-buried-the-national-debate-with-logical-fallacies/

Topping, S. (2018). Biography of Joseph Pulitzer. http://www.pulitzer.org/page/biography-joseph-pulitzer

Wang, G. & Hackett, R. (2020). Virtues-centered moral identity: An identity-based explanation of the functioning of virtuous leadership. *The Leadership Quarterly. 31*(5).

Waszak, E. & Bean, E. (2019). Ethan's healthy mind express: A children's first mental health primer. *EBMWF*

Whitlock, C. (2019). At war with the truth. https://www.washingtonpost.com/graphics/2019/investigations/afghanistan-papers/afghanistan-war-confidential-documents/

Ventura, J. & Russell, D. (2021). 63 documents that government doesn't want you to read. Skyhorse imprint of Simon & Schuster.

Appendix: Bias Assessment Form

How objective are you and how objective is the piece you assess? The higher the partiality score, the more bias the piece exhibits. It is virtually impossible to remove all bias from any published materials. This form is based on your rating to 9 key questions and assessing KLEMP. All questions — aside from documenting if the published piece can be found in a library database, as well as ethos and mythos — can be assessed within the piece itself. Your ability to assess is tied to your desire to be objective. The final rating will place the piece as either Extreme Bias, High Bias, **Bias**, Low Bias, and Very Low Bias. **Caution should be used if you follow and share information in the Extreme and High Bias categories.**

Title: _____ Author/Entity _____
Publication Date _ _/_ _/_ _ Bias Source Tied To > ____ Academic ___ Hidden Agenda
____ For-Profit ____ Non-Profit ____ Watchdog Group ____ Government ____ Individual

USE CRITICAL THINKING TO ASSESS PUBLISHED PIECE FOR CONTENT IN RELATION TO POTENTIAL BIAS SOURCE CHECKED ABOVE:

1. The piece cannot be identified as a bonafide journalistic source (Chapter 4).
True = 1, False = 0 Score ___

2. The published piece is designed to be an Editorial or Blog.
True = 1, False = 0 Score ___

3. The published piece CANNOT be found in a library database.
True = 1, False = 0 Score ___

For 4 to 8: 1 to 5 scale, 5 = yes or most
1 = little or none

4. Rate the extent to whether you believe the piece exhibits sensationalism.
1 2 3 4 5   Score ___

5. To what extent do you believe the piece exhibits a Hidden Agenda?
1 2 3 4 5   Score ___

6. Does the author or entity associated with the published piece have a conflict of interest that interferes with its objectivity?
1 2 3 4 5   Score ___

7. To what extent do you believe any of the 10 possible fallacies exists within the piece?
1 2 3 4 5   Score ___

8. To what extent do your personal biases or hasty generalization impede your ability to objectively analyze the piece? 1 2 3 4 5   Score ___

Tally Questions 1-8 Score ___ of 28

9. Assess KLEMP (Rate Accordingly)

Kairos: Publication is more than 1 month old.
True (1)   False (0)   Score ___

Logos: Publication is not factual, does not contain valid attribution and lacks citations and/or quotes.
1 2 3 4 5 < Not Factual   Score ___

Ethos: Based on researching the author's background, does the published piece provide too much of the author's own bias or lack of humanity to be objective?

1 2 3 4 5 < Higher Bias   Score ___

Mythos: Again, based on researching the author's Subject Matter Expertise (SME) does the published piece provide too much of the author's own bias or lack of humanity to be objective?

1 2 3 4 5 < Higher Bias   Score ___

Pathos: Rate the information for the level of emotion it contains.(5 = high emotion, 1 = little)

1 2 3 4 5 < High Emotion Score ___

Final KLEMP   Score ___ of 21
Q. 1-8 Assessment   + ___ of 28
   TOTAL PARTIALITY SCORE ___ of 49

___ **40 to 49** Extreme Bias
___ **30 to 39** High Bias
___ **20 to 29 Bias**
___ **10 to 19** Low Bias
___ **01 to 09** Very Low Bias

Bias Is All Around You

ABOUT THE CONTRIBUTORS

ERIK BEAN

Erik holds a master's degree in journalism from Michigan State University and he also holds a doctorate in education with sanctioned research interests in cultural competence, leadership, and mental health. A section editor of *The Journal of*  *Leadership Studies*, John Wiley & Sons, he also is founder of the Ethan Bean Mental Wellness Foundation, a Michigan 501(c)3 public charity. Other recent book projects include the award-winning *Ethan's Healthy Mind Express: A Children's First Mental Health Primer* and co-author of the self-help series 20/20 Prudent Leadership.

GAIL GORSKE

Illustrator Gail Gorske is a master paper art professional whose award-winning illustrations include nature photography and those found in *Ethan's Healthy Mind Express* and the *20/20 Prudent Leadership* book series. Her images have inspired generations to critically think and cross all boundaries of race, religion, gender, and nationalities.

SHERRY WEXLER

Editor Sherry Wexler holds an L.M.S.W. She is a graduate of Wayne State University. Her editing work includes the award-winning book *Ethan's Healthy Mind Express*.

TIM VOS

With over 4,000 citations referencing his work on Gatekeeping Theory, journalism's role in democracy, and media criticism, foreword contributor, Dr. Vos is director of the School of Journalism, Michigan State University.

Web: HealthyMindExpress.org
Web This Title: BiasHandbook.com
Email: info@ethanbean.org
Phone: (248) 270-2974